Patterns: A Bard's Midnight Verse

Nana Kwame Sakyi

BookLeaf
Publishing

India | USA | UK

Presentation by *BookLeaf Publishing*

Web: www.bookleafpub.com

E-mail: info@bookleafpub.com

ISBN: 9789360943615

First edition 2024

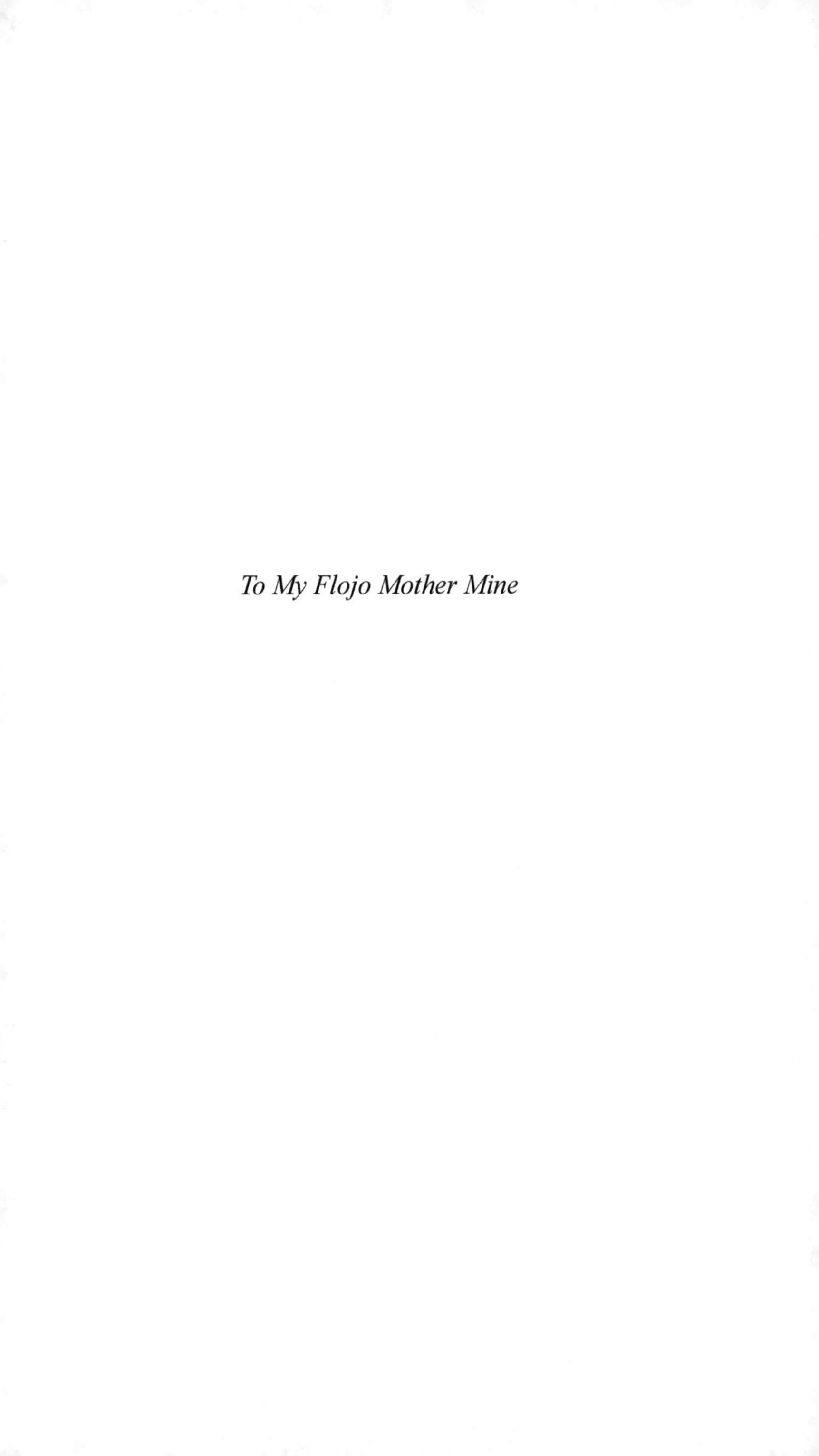

To My Flojo Mother Mine

A Mustard Dream

Dreams are trees
Oaks or teaks
As tall as deep
Forth in the thicket of ideals
Spitesome when shoot
Belle once crowned with bloom
And ah, the sky at last -
Not only soul to thrill
Even the coo-coos in their foliage
Do us remind
Diadems are fitless on dreamless heads

Dreams are seeds
Mustard I deem
A toss down the deep,
And the couple --- heart and hand
Pampers the baby soil
As the dream makes ready to die
Well aware today is no day to lie
Yet knowing death is the very life:
A life watered by the laws of desire
Thirstily skimmed off such dry-eyed clouds
And alas! A skyline of teal canopy

Dreams are keys

Keys to doors
Doors of fulfilment
A fulfilment of call
The call in a man
One lot for each
Each one for all
All spared but once
What then to say:
A dream is key
If a seed be tree

The Re-Defector

She's a tot kangaroo
Who wandered from the pouch
Into a skippy haven;
He's a two-inch nail
Who the drowsy field did protest
And kicked 'gainst a half-filled basin;
That's a wanderlust falcon
Wanton for fair meat
But chanced upon a cheetah's game;
I'm an ageless phoenix
Who taught but thought foul
And now dread the ash insurrection.

'Tis our nameless faun only
Who served golden noodles
And will never spoon-feed us
Jesting our green appetites;
Then, not to hurt our inky feelings,
Mutter away in cussed defiance:
'Even when Ashanti teaspoons I gift…
Glory not… 'tis a teaspoon I give'
Unloved, who cared!

Nigh we stroll…
 unmoved, while he sleeps

in the snow…
the grin in his teeth;
now I only beg to buy time
for if speech be cheap,
chief is spendthrift
and luxury, cheap

And…
I'm not one who knows not
a kinsman-redeemer true, but…

Loner with Nix

Tonight, 'neath her blind air, I go my way
Cheerlessly fade away from thee mi love,
Saunter off to a cheer clad far away
Drawn away by the twilit street above…,
Nay, my love wanest not nor hath new found –
Needless to say, mine heart wouldst you not go
For whe'er thy love, thy pleasures abound,
Nor do thou merit a come-uppance so
beastly and costly. 'Tis all to my shame:
I hushed up to a sepulchral breather
what now calleth me yon to trade love's fame:
the husbandry of debauched souls – preacher…
cheerio mi love, lest we bewitch our feet
fate accomplish'd, ne'er the twain shall met.

In Praise of Kamau

In the picturesque volcanic mounds
… my blood bother Kamau –
A son of the Great Rift Valley
A crest I smooch now an' then
I espouse to thee mine heart
Why…?
Why – he flung burning spears
and stomped, hoity-toity, on Mau Mau
Surpassing Shylock's pound of flesh;
He blatantly shooed the natives home;
And got coal and water flaring
He yet persisted…

… my black brother Kamau;
Black, aye. Slack, nay.
He thrives in the barren throes
And still catches game
In the wake of The Judge's trod
The threadbare tartan pounds
With known harambee strides
Et al panting on his trail

… my boisterous brother Kamau;
In a mighty surge of muscle,
He poaches friends of the tusk;

The soil, tilled with glee,
His tender coffee hands you see
'neath a comely blanket of stars,
On him rests the onus of an onerous dance
And done, you loathe him not once

… Kamau, my Kikuyu blood brother;
A warrior in heart and art
A stork at sight yet eagle alright
Aye! Jamhuri ya Kamau;
'Tis ope, prithee, come hither
Aye! Kamau Mwigithania
In their faces, I sing your praise

Eureka!

If you strive hard enough
To dream all you can;
And look far enough
To do all you can,
You shall come to it
And chance upon your dream;
And eureka! You are there!

Then shall I see you
The sight of you upstream;
The joy to feel
The cares you'll conceal;
Then only will you know
The tales of the unknown;
And eureka! You'll be free to scream.

Focus it through the Light
And stand inspite the strife;
He is the end to the means
And key to your being;
Then, when on a golden stool you sit
Thus, have you wandered to it;
And eureka! You have it!

The Tempest

How thou be swungen O my soul
When shalt thou stay thy sway
For thou art bereft of thy sole
Doth it not stir thee
That thy joys be long gone assail
Whither shalt thou be furlong sunken
And shamed before thy foes
To be sound bound and found wanton
And tu-whooed by nights so cold
Fix not thine eyes save beyond this isle
From whence standeth lone the goodly tree
For though thy wound be deep, festering vile
Thy praise singes are few and far between
O grieve not thy tears nor frazzled sigh
Your cloud is but sun, and the rain her sons
Only be of good cheer; morn draweth nigh
When vengeance shall be sweet as acapella
And thou shalt chew laughter with Muscatella

God's Isle

Mi-self, a guest of His starry host
Lost in an old-fashion'd silver cloud,
My respectful hand guarded a calabashful
Of fresh frothy palm wine
On its way for a sip,
The other hewn back and forth
A raffia fan;
Then…my eyes beheld God's Isle
That He longed I saw awhile.

Lo, 'twas like…
Like a giant-fisted dome of sunken fufu
In a May-9th nkrakra overwhelm;
Hemmed in by a blind stampede
Of tender goatmeat trampling one on another
Betwixt and between a winsome squad
Of hard-boiled eggs;
Sure to incur a referee's wrath
Or harvest goals foul wrought:

Charm bereav'd, the air mute,
God was bemused;
I just caught His eyes,
Bore through them, but
Stray'd my stare:

For there… in the right one –
Its duct let go a tear
That he forbade I saw;
My calabash straightway held dread
That my throat would dredge.

Oh I feared that I feared not
Right in the presence of His lot
When my eyes beheld God's Isle
That He longed I saw awhile.

December-tide

On birth sheets death pee drips
And in them lie raw glimpses
Of life that never may die
And the whole of mine is behind mine eyes
Holding true some relish down time
Tasting the tang of many memories ago
When the green skies were too young
To demand harvest from the red
And cracking palms of the tan-skins
That owned them;

When in the wind-swept high tide
The shea fruit
paid up the moisture loss
With her pure truth
Of natural gloss
Accentuating solid silhouettes of soil –
That golden staying oil;

When the plains in golden grays a-lay
And the cotton fields
No longer held bread
In the singeing threats
Of the Ancient Keeper of day;

When at high season
Feet pell-mell grew
In the once disdainful market-places
And clansmen we almost knew
In thousand surfaced with longing faces;

When we then, a penn'orth of pans surround
And with scant culinary skill
Did open a white tin can
And devoured the hallowed canned things;

Oh with sheer certainty we knew
'Adwoa-Yankees' will flatter our black sorts
And make us blush playing the caroller –
Yet 'twas pure mirth we sought
When we welcomed a fresh Yule
From the fraying twigs of December

Patterns

All we know, same has been
After birth the after-birth
All these eyes have seen
Have been for a time, times and half a time
But when death do us part
Our hearts go on
Go on the novel voyage
Go a-sail the seventh sea
Reach down and touch the depths
Reach up and kiss the clouds
Reach yon to heal deep wounds
Reach out to wipe all tears
So how I let all things go!
For flavour to the nose sounds sweet
And to the lips fragrance is sweeter still
But none is nowise game for the other
Here then we merely meet to part

Thereon, naked as truth
Bearing no gifts
Only born anew
On the sauntered street
Barely thinking nor sorting
Just onward keeping
For how long, an idle fathom

Airborne, you bid farewell to the midlands
Revelling alone in her pesky earthy pride
But you with much forbearance
(Much more than you could bear)
Strut forwards beside the smart aides
Amid matchless cheers:
Ahoy there! Bravo mon frere!
Hallo affendi! Oh, whoopee!
Akwaaba o! Ayeekoo o!
a-a-a-a-a-a-a-a-h-h-h-h-h
you breathe deep in all the fair
(inspite the grim-faced retreating train
Careening down the way we head
Looking like the spent night-sky
Starved of moonlight)
You'll never know such pure fresh air
Till you're 'neath the dome
Lonely with no friend nor caregiver

Unattended and so short of breath
You'll then be free
Free to know the bliss
This bliss I know with no learning
Just an insatiable yearning
(a steep deep longing)
For mountains to peak
That valleys may be
An with it a labyrinth of watery alleyways
And a range of flowery gaze

Where you can perch on the peak
Overlooking the glassy sea
Gleaming as a cleaned-clean looking glass –
The breathwork of the cherubic geisha
Clad in the sweet-pea patterned kimono –
The handiwork of the fancy-fingered fabric
freak

And underneath the watery deep
Your jelly eyes will find
The unraped flora
And the virgin breasts of the sea;
A peek above your head,
And the bright beams beat your brow
And your best day is born
When you behold the stunning stunts
Of the manifold winged compatriots
All dressed in petticoats
With no glory-sorry songs
Up their comely beaks

And o-o-h you can set faith free
And soar far beyond the farthest horizon
Plant a full-lipped kiss
On the moon's wet left cheek
And still go on
To cup a handful of the honey
Dripping down the excited horn of Africa;

There, upon a thousand thousands
You still find silver adds no gold to soul
As the unshifting sights of sounds
From the Holy City flatters you with such
sweetness
One eternal moment after another

Atop It All

How strange the feeling
How great the tingling
Glaring up the awesome spray of Falls
Praying you'd be atop it all
Yet 'neath there you sit entranced or enraged
Dead to dare to try
But if you'll find the will
To pull through impossible doors
You the scoffers' back will break
When in the plenteous plunder you rake
You'll reap cheers for tears
Where faith was sown to spite the fear
Then many heads a-step –
Enthroned on the glorious arch
With colours aplenty
You can rhyme the smile
Rippling across the Nile

About My Dream

No-one ever said 'twas all easy
For then all men would be at ease
And all of us shall sweatless be there
I've so much longed this tread
Many times imagined hitting the goal
Very much seen that end
Many times in my dreams

Haughty witnesses wish I'd cry
Doubting thoughts prey upon my mind
Sorry times oft have been my wine;
So many ends mine eyes have seen
While I pry this unpopular corner:
Being a living sacrifice
With a fire blazing inside
Where great men have trodden
The great still shall near
O'er and o'er and o'er again
Contrary winds yet against
Till the end of all things –
When humanity shall cease;
While the while the sun must rouse with delight
And catch a west wind home by night

So there's no need to cry

There's really no need for tears
For my comfort is nigh
Inspite the fears;
In all these cares
Armed with life anew
I live because of You

Transitions

Ain't gonna be long
…lest we forget to play
Play life as we ought
Lest we forget the passionate flames
…singing the love of death
Celebrating her lovers in debt

Arcanum arcanorum
…secrets of secrets
Love will unravel death's mystique
The lone traveller dare not contrast so
…so to contest living scores
Hidden enroute the chaste abyss
…holding up sapiens' zipped psalter:
Entrapment of the sepulchre

Testy flames
…sullen sails yet a-sail
Against the will
Yet with none to still
Fight! Fight!
Stage a good fight!
O thirsty flames thou must feed
Elude so…odasani, flee!

Fission

Spurt! Squirt! Squash! Splasssh!
…rush hour
Upstream, downstream, jet-steam
Our resilient right-hand strikes

Affendi, 'tis upon you!
It flows: It's thick
It's dreadful and dark:
Sun-scorched, ash burnt
Blood, fire and billows of smoke

Art and nature; –
The perfect fusion
…of the beautiful and useful
This hour in shiftless nadir

Genteel moon beams gone berserk
Shaggy clouds of wrath
Peaks clad in pomposity
Under the cloak of mere visibility,
Peak to heaps – rubble

Meditations, memoirs of silence
Maranatha!

Snapshot from a Haiku Boat
(Haiku Verse)

Ere black-bliss nightfall
Dusk atop a rig ashore
Dare a dawn chorus

On genteel tide
The rare oyster-buster rides
Still, on a kelp rock

From the domed crowning
A dream crow a-cawing
In a swaying palm

Down on sandy beach
Ah, this drunk for same palm reach
To stay bottled thoughts

Social Chronicle

O these clueless ones I see
Acclaimed to be in a queue;
Sparsely a-break all over
When she's next he trumps over:
This mere needless linear wreck
Mirrors what a mental mess
Smothers our society so

Tonight

Tonight the blinking of the stars
Fades with the black laughter
Swathed across the sky
And the silvery sweet spies
Untwinkle too
Justified by the hollow stare
In the ball of the night's eye –
Stupefied of all
By the cloudless beauty tonight;
And the silence…, shh has no equal
The real lady she is…
Careful not to rouse the living deadness
While tolerating the twitters
Of the galivanting crickets
And… the leapfrogged deafness;
But with no wheeze in the trees
This fear fetters the fair:
The unwelcome warmth tonight

My Beloved and I Tonight

To be a man was easy then:
Proof of which was easier still –
A dainty black bruise over Obaa Yaa's brow
And Papa had one damn good omen
Over and away in his grave clothes

'Tis all so beautiful
I hear the rhythmic chinking across the darkness
Not for once mistaken for a seah of seed
Let loose upon the ready bed
Nor of Awo's (mother) tired gray hands either
That'd spilled again the morrows peas
Across the sun-beaten yard;
No, 'twas a far lovelier noise
A melody well known to me only
The sweet beckoning of the golden brown pod:
The cultured seed of the red-earth oven
That without learning, I know, is down upon
The flawless waistline of the silhouetted beau
Who lends the moonlit night a charm
It never shall possess of her own

Yes, 'tis the velvety voice of my beloved now at
hand
And straightway, I know

The secret place we shall steal away to tonight
Away from the loveless eyes
Of the so-called city suitors;
We shall escape into her warm embrace –
O thee mighty baobab of love;
It all comes to me like 'twas just yesternight:
O how we played all night
Under her showy umbrella
The plenty moonlight here and there
Prancing gleefully in the sea of sand
That adorns her 'stablshed feet;
I still feel her scented breath on mine
As I run my probing fingers along the pure lustre
Of her flowing braids

I could forever stay my stare
Into her dark tan eyes divinely set
In a chocolatey face well glossed over
With the balmy acquaintance of the harmattan;
And how we would smell each other
Was all we longed to do
My beloved and I Tonight;
Mine eyes as yet may not see
The mysteries 'neath the well patterned
Wrapper draped across her full bosom –
The bride price will tell the rest of the tale

Obunumankoma's (The Almighty's) nightbird
will tell

When we emerge from these thyme trees
Once again tonight…
So filled with the wine of ecstasy
Yes, she will tell if we did a thing more:
That was our game
A game we so played with no shame
A game well forgotten inspite her fame
So who dares now give it what name
With no red roses we dined alright
With no glory-sorry songs
We danced to the flattering tune of silence:
I daresay my beloved knows a cheer more
Than the pittance of icy rosettes you gift Shakira
Just for a piece of her waist

KENTE

Kro-kro-kro-kro-he-he-he-he
Kro-he-kro-he-kro-kro-kro…
The master beaver at work:
Weaving the unseen intricacies
Of the simple seen together
Pooling up all that goes asunder:
Making wise the simple
To confound the wise,
The wild and tame and tilled;
O what divine design

Kro-kro-kro-kro-he-he-he-he
Kro-he-kro-he-kro-kro-kro…
Shuttles shuffling side to side
Design doth develop down and up;
Click clapping click
Cluttered cloven yarns
Climax in cloying coloured cloth

Stilled, the earthen spool spins
To feed the loom a meal
Of warp with colour
To whet the weft of fibre;
And the jealous whines
At the bit of such design

Whites smilin'
Yellows yellin'
Greens greetin'
Gold glows to give
The weaver a web of wonder
KENTE: The miracle of Bonwire

From the voiceless tradition of patterns
Emanates Adinkra: the Eloquent Duke
The rhythmic burr of the loom
*Adinkrahene aSankofa
Owuo Atwede3 ama Adwinasa…
Gye Nyame!
This rhythm of life:
The legacy of Ananse
The phantom by the fireside
The false face who possesses,
The web of secrets
The secrets of Kente
The secret of life
The very verse of God

Can one embrace the warmth of Kente
And not be smitten with love;
Can one be blind to the Designer
Sitting above the circle of the earth
In the surpassing excellences of nature;
Will such an inspired harmony

Pull on the unruly cords of discord
In this dignified culture of purity;

Kente knows the truth
The infernal truth of oneness –
Unity in diversity;
Kente holds the key
Enshrouded in poisoned blackmail;
Is it heresy? In every white lies black
And in them shall none lack –
The idyll of life:
KENTE
O thee unsung hero!

*(A play of words, to wit:
But for God, all hell will break loose,
For the King of Adinkra
Has brought back the ladder of death)

O She-lumber by the Roadside

There she stands more like Shiloh
Beside the ash of cooled tar
Home bound to esCape the Coast

Red dirt chasing at the wheels
Wheeze past her, beating her sore
Yet the stalwart just won't wince

While her folks catch on the cold
Distraught, graying by the day
Solid bulwark still she stands
Sanctuary for the beloved bird

O you make me go six sevens
O she-lumber by the roadside

A Neighbour Comes By

That the Psalmist was tempted is human
That he triumphed is rather divine
Can see the rainbow in my cup
Inspite the unchristening feel
Where all the soul is stewed in the bitter hush
When the sun is down and done for
And the filled shadows steal away from the
suitor
After a neighbour comes by…
Just to turn in a g'day
And to show his gratitude
For your kindness on Sunday

Allere Flammam (Feed the Flame)

Comerades, its about that time
When the gazelle pursues
The lords of the wild
Full with passionate strength
Stronger than the Lions of Teranga

Time when flame-warm blood
Turn womb-men henchmen o' war
Where yesterdays' illusion dies
And dreams dock ashore
Time when strange bedfellows do fly
And battles won are fought

The scented aroma barren countryside craves
Basks up in the presence of rain
The stench of death recedes
Lo, the women's dead are receiv'd;
Where the battle is fiercest
There abides the fearless

Comerades, its about that time
When prayers are prayed
Void of the charade upstage
Where fire hails down

And glory ascends from the victory chants –
Yea, heavens' gates part for our dance

spirits succumb to the Great Spirit
Oil is outpoured upon vessels of honour and
dishonour
Verdant grass in sparks sweat
Drenched in earth's dawn trot
Paradise lost restored
We're moving up to the highest places

Woes and goals in one moment
Fruitless and fertile harvested same day
No need for swords nor plowshares
Mind not the hourglass nor arment
Time and works go no further
Only eternal wives hereafter
This is to all in Megiddo
Who suck on in sainted slumber
Not meet for the morrows' Armageddon